Now and then

Clothes

Monica Hughes

Heinemann
LIBRARY

Little Nippers

www.heinemann.co.uk/library
Visit our website to find out more information about **Heinemann Library** books.

To order:
☎ Phone 44 (0) 1865 888066
▤ Send a fax to 44 (0) 1865 314091
▭ Visit the Heinemann Bookshop at www.heinemann.co.uk/library to browse our
   catalogue and order online.

First published in Great Britain by Heinemann Library, Halley Court, Jordan Hill, Oxford OX2 8EJ, part of Harcourt Education. Heinemann is a registered trademark of Harcourt Education Ltd.

Editorial: Sarah Eason and Georga Godwin
Design: Jo Hinton-Malivoire and Tokay, Bicester, UK (www.tokay.co.uk)
Picture Research: Rosie Garai and Debra Weatherley
Production: Edward Moore

Originated by Dot Gradations Ltd
Printed and bound in China by South China Printing Company

ISBN 0 431 18643 X (hardback)
07 06 05 04 03
10 9 8 7 6 5 4 3 2 1

ISBN 0 431 18648 0 (paperback)
07 06 05 04 03
10 9 8 7 6 5 4 3 2 1

British Library Cataloguing in Publication Data
Hughes, Monica
Now and Then – Clothes
391'.009
A full catalogue record for this book is available from the British Library.

Acknowledgements
The Publishers would like to thank the following for permission to reproduce photographs:
Alamy Images **p. 11**; Bubbles/Frans Rombout **p. 16**; Bubbles/Loisjoy Thurstun **p. 22**; Corbis/Ariel Skelley **p. 4**; Corbis/Chris Carroll **p. 6**; Corbis/Rolf Bruderer **p. 8**; Getty Images **pp. 13**, **15**, **17**, **19**, **23**; Getty Images/Hulton Archive **p. 5**; John Walmsley **p. 18**; Mary Evans Picture Library **p. 7**; Popperfoto **pp. 9**, **21**; Steve Behr **pp. 10**, **12**; Trip/S. Hill **p. 14**; Tudor Photography **p. 20**.

Cover photograph reproduced with permission of Getty Images/Hulton Archive.

The Publishers would like to thank Annie Davy for her assistance in the preparation of this book.

Every effort has been made to contact copyright holders of any material reproduced in this book. Any omissions will be rectified in subsequent printings if notice is given to the Publishers.

Contents

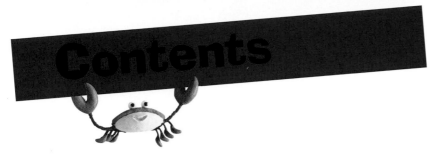

Colours of clothes

Now clothes are lots of different colours.

Are these clothes the same as yours?

Then

Jackets and coats

We love our cosy **padded** jackets.

Now

What would it be like to wear coats like these?

Then

Shorts and trousers

Now

Look at all the different kinds of shorts.

Short trousers were once really short!

Then

Sweaters and jumpers

Sweatshirts are very **comfortable** now.

Then

Lots of jumpers were hand knitted and sometimes **itchy!**

Shoes and boots

Now

Which of these shoes and boots would you like to wear?

Then

Hats

Now

Hats to keep off the Sun.

14

Hats to keep out the cold.

Then

Night wear

Look at the clothes we go to sleep in now.

Then

Do these clothes
look as **comfortable**?

School uniforms

Now

Which uniform would you like to wear?

New clothes

Now most clothes are bought in shops.

Washing clothes

Now machines can **wash** and **dry** clothes.

Then

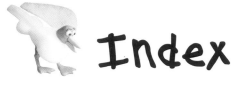

Index

Notes for adults

This series supports the child's knowledge and understanding of their world, in particular their personal, social and emotional development. The following Early Learning Goals are relevant to the series:

• make connections between different parts of their life experience
• show an awareness of change
• begin to differentiate between past and present
• introduce language that enables them to talk about their experiences in greater depth and detail.

It is important to relate the **Now** photographs to the child's own experiences and so help them differentiate between the past and present. The **Then** photographs can be introduced by using phrases like: *When I was your age, When granddad was a boy, Before you were born*. By comparing the two photographs they can begin to identify similarities and differences between the present and the past. Ask open-ended questions like: Do you remember when …? What might it be like …? What do you think …? This will help the child to develop their own ideas and extend their thinking.

Many of the basic items of clothing shown in the **Then** photographs will be immediately familiar to the child. There may be changes to the type of materials used, the colours available and the variety of designs. The child can be encouraged to identify some of these and to think about the effect this might have had on the wearer.

A follow up activity could include drawing **Then/Now** pictures of things that are now similar for both girls & boys and those that were once quite different.